Intermediate to Advanced Piano Solo

THE WORLD'S GREAT CLA

MW00785365

Piano Prelu~~~

63 Preludes by 16 Composers from the Baroque to the 20th Century

EDITED BY TIMOTHY SCHORR

Cover Painting: Pierre-Auguste Renoir, *Yvonne and Christine Lerolle at the Piano*, 1897
Musée d'Orsay, Paris, France   Oil on canvas

ISBN 0-634-08712-6

7777 W. BLUEMOUND RD. P.O. BOX 13819 MILWAUKEE, WI 53213

In Australia Contact:
Hal Leonard Australia Pty. Ltd.
4 Lentara Court
Cheltenham, Victoria, 3192 Australia
Email: ausadmin@halleonard.com

Visit Hal Leonard Online at
www.halleonard.com

CONTENTS

Isaac Albéniz 8 Preludio from *Cantos de España*, Op. 232, No. 1

17 Preludio from *España*, Op. 165, No. 1

Charles Valentin Alkan 20 Prelude in B Major, Op. 31, No. 23

Johann Sebastian Bach from *12 Little Preludes:*

22 Little Prelude No. 3 in C Minor

25 Little Prelude No. 4 in D Major

26 Little Prelude No. 11 in G Minor

from *The Well-Tempered Clavier, Book I:*

28 Prelude in C Major

34 Prelude in C Minor

38 Prelude in D Major

31 Prelude in D Minor

42 Prelude in G Major

44 Prelude in G Minor

from *The Well-Tempered Clavier, Book II:*

46 Prelude in C Major

49 Prelude in D Major

54 Prelude in D Minor

57 Prelude in F Minor

Ludwig van Beethoven 60 Two Preludes through All Major Keys, Op. 39

Ferruccio Busoni 72 Prelude in D-flat Major, Op. 37, No. 15

75 Prelude in F-sharp Minor, Op. 37, No. 8

Fryderyk Chopin 78 Prelude in A-flat Major, Op. 28, No. 17

83 Prelude in A Major, Op. 28, No. 7

84 Prelude in B Minor, Op. 28, No. 6

86 Prelude in C Minor, Op. 28, No. 20

87 Prelude in C-sharp Minor, Op. 45

92 Prelude in D-flat Major, Op. 28, No. 15

98 Prelude in E Major, Op. 28, No. 9

102 Prelude in E Minor, Op. 28, No. 4

99 Prelude in F-sharp Major, Op. 28, No. 13

104 Prelude in G Minor, Op. 28, No. 22

François Couperin from *L'art de toucher le Clavecin:*

106 Third Prelude

108 Eighth Prelude

Claude Debussy   from *Préludes, Book I:*
                              111   La Cathédrale engloutie
                              116   Des pas sur la neige
                              118   La fille aux cheveux de lin
                              124   Minstrels

                                    from *Préludes, Book II:*
                              128   Bruyères
                              121   Canope

George Frideric Handel   132   Prelude from Suite in D Minor, HG II/i/3
                              134   Prelude from Suite in E Major, HG II/i/5
                              136   Prelude from Suite in F Minor, HG II/i/8

Johann Ludwig Krebs   138   Prelude No. 3 in E Minor
                              146   Prelude No. 5 in G Major

Felix Mendelssohn   from *Six Preludes and Fugues*, Op. 35:
                              148   Prelude No. 4 in A-flat Major
                              152   Prelude No. 5 in F Minor
                              156   Prelude No. 6 in B-flat Major

Sergei Prokofiev   141   Prelude, Op. 12, No. 7

Henry Purcell   160   Prelude from Suite in C Major, Z. 666
                              162   Prelude from Suite in G Major, Z. 662
                              164   Prelude from Suite in G Minor, Z. 661

Sergei Rachmaninoff   166   Prelude in C-sharp Minor, Op. 3, No. 2
                              172   Prelude in D Major, Op. 23, No. 4
                              176   Prelude in E-flat Major, Op. 23, No. 6
                              180   Prelude in G Major, Op. 32, No. 5
                              185   Prelude in G Minor, Op. 23, No. 5
                              192   Prelude in G-sharp Minor, Op. 32, No. 12

Clara Schumann   197   Prelude No. 2 in B-flat Major from Three Preludes and Fugues, Op. 16

Alexander Skryabin   200   Prelude for the Left Hand in C-sharp Minor, Op. 9, No. 1
                              202   Prelude in A Minor, Op. 11, No. 2
                              206   Prelude in B-flat Major, Op. 35, No. 2
                              205   Prelude in C-sharp Minor, Op. 22, No. 2
                              208   Prelude in E Major, Op. 11, No. 9
                              210   Prelude in G Major, Op. 11, No. 3
                              212   Prelude in G-sharp Minor, Op. 22, No. 1

ABOUT THE COMPOSERS...

ISAAC ALBÉNIZ (1860-1909)

Paving the way for Spanish piano music, Isaac Albéniz got his start as a pianist at the tender age of four when he performed at the Teatro Romea in Barcelona to a bewildered audience. After being denied admission to the Paris Conservatoire for being "too young," Albéniz ran away from home at age 12 and traveled alone as a stowaway through South America, Cuba, Puerto Rico and his native Spain. In the 1880s, he followed Franz Liszt on a tour through Eastern Europe, all along polishing his piano skills. Later, in Paris, he befriended such great French masters as Debussy, d'Indy, Fauré and Dukas. Albéniz is most known for his masterpiece *Suite Iberia* for piano, composed near the end of his life in France. Spanish folk music provided a strong foundation for the majority of Albéniz's work. Teamed with the mutual influence of his French counterparts, he contributed to the birth of the impressionist style in music. In addition to piano music, he also composed for the theatre, orchestra and voice.

CHARLES VALENTIN ALKAN (1813-1888)

French child prodigy and virtuoso pianist, Charles Valentin Alkan was first published when he was 14 years old. Onetime close friend of Chopin and George Sand, he soon withdrew from social circles, leading a solitary life while teaching at the Paris Conservatoire. Despite the praise of such luminaries as Busoni, Cherubini and Liszt, Alkan's music was not well known in either his time or by succeeding generations. It is likely that his music was better known from publications than performance. He took long recesses from the concert stage often amounting to more than 20 years at a time. When he did perform it was usually the music of composers other than himself. As a pianist, he preferred strict rhythmic precision rather than the rubato style of the period. His compositions were influenced by such old masters as Bach and Handel as well as the music of his contemporaries, mainly Chopin. Although the majority of his compositions were for the piano, he also composed works for orchestra, chamber ensemble and voice.

JOHANN SEBASTIAN BACH (1685-1750)

Johann Sebastian Bach's incomparable genius for musical form and structure is revered more than 300 years after his birth. Yet the Baroque master and his music were actually forgotten by the general public and musicians alike for many years. Musical fashions were already changing by Bach's later years, and his music was heard less frequently than earlier in his lifetime. After his death, which may have been hastened by treatments and surgery for blindness, his music fell out of fashion. His second wife, Anna Magdelena, died in poverty about ten years later. Bach's works span a wide range of genres. He wrote liturgical works, Lutheran masses, church and secular cantatas, chamber music, organ works, orchestral pieces, concertos, vocal and choral pieces as well as compositions for clavier. In his day he was widely known as a virtuoso organist. His improvisational skills were legendary. With his contemporary George Frideric Handel, whom he never met, he was one of the last great composers of the Baroque era. Some ninety years after Bach's death, his works were once again brought before the public by the composer and conductor Felix Mendelssohn. Mendelssohn became a champion of the works of Bach and other composers who had been pushed aside with the shifting of musical fashions. Bach's music has been a mainstay of the international repertoire ever since.

LUDWIG VAN BEETHOVEN (1770-1827)

It is difficult to know how much of our perception of Beethoven is myth and how much is fact. He was the greatest composer of his era, certainly. Beethoven began his musical studies with his father, a Bonn court musician. He was appointed as deputy court organist in Bonn when he was eleven years old. He later continued his studies with Haydn, until differences between the two ended their relationship. Beethoven was first known to the public as a brilliant, flamboyant piano virtuoso, but there was a much darker aspect to his life. He was devastated when, in his late teens, he was summoned home from Vienna to keep vigil at his mother's deathbed. The second great tragedy of his life began when he was quite young, as a slight hearing impairment. Then in 1802, when the composer was 32, he was informed by doctors that he would eventually lose his hearing altogether. Beethoven sank into a deep despair, during which he wrote a will of sorts to his brothers. Whether or not he was considering suicide is a subject of some speculation. Whatever the case, the "Heiligenstadt Testament," as the will is known, states that he believed he would soon be dead. He eventually came to terms with his deafness and went on to write some of his most powerful pieces. His last six symphonies were written in the following years. In addition to his nine symphonies, Beethoven wrote pieces in nearly every imaginable genre. His works include an oratorio, two ballets, an opera, incidental music for various theatrical productions, military music, cantatas, a wealth of chamber music, 32 piano sonatas, various piano pieces, some 85 songs and 170 folksong arrangements. At Beethoven's funeral, on March 29, 1827, some 10,000 people joined in his funeral procession. One of the torch-bearers was composer Franz Schubert, who had idolized Beethoven. Some 45 years after his funeral, Beethoven's body was moved to Vienna's Central Cemetery, where he lies near the grave of Schubert.

FERRUCCIO BUSONI (1866-1924)

Born to a professional clarinettist and a pianist, Ferruccio Busoni was a child prodigy on the piano. Following his early compositional studies in Austria with Wilhelm Mayer, Busoni moved back to his native Italy to attend the Accademia filarmonica in Bologna. By the age of 20 he moved to Leipzig where he met such prominent composers as Mahler, Delius, Grieg and Tchaikovsky. Having already become famous for his pianistic virtuosity in Vienna, Busoni went on to study composition at the Helsinki Conservatory with Sibelius. In the early 1890s he went to New York and Boston to pursue a concert pianist career. Although his music never broke the barriers of tonality in the same way as Schoenberg, Busoni's music and theory had a significant impact on the development of modern music, especially that of Varèse. In addition to performing, composing and theorizing, Busoni was also a gifted transcriber of the music of Bach. He was a teacher, and conductor, a champion of compositions by Delius, Bartók, Debussy, Franck, Fauré, d'Indy and Sibelius. His *Elegien* for piano marks a clear shift in his development as a composer. Obsessed with his new ideas about "universal music," he worked feverishly at adapting Goethe's *Faust* as an opera. Left unfinished at his death due to the rage of war and ill-health, *Doktor Faust* was completed and produced by his friend Philipp Jarnach in 1925.

FRYDERYK CHOPIN (1810-1849)

Although composer and pianist Fryderyk Chopin was born to a French father and spent half of his life in Paris, he always defined himself by the land of his birth, Poland. Throughout his life he retained strong nationalistic feelings. Chopin the pianist achieved the status of an idol. His mystique was based in part on his cultured upbringing and in part on his fragile good looks. His sensitive nature, frail health, and self-imposed exile only intensified the public's fascination with him. In 1831, after receiving his training and achieving some success in Poland, Chopin moved to Paris. There he found himself one of many piano virtuosos. Although he quickly made a name for himself, his temperament and physical frailty, caused by tuberculosis that plagued him throughout much of his life, left him poorly suited to life as a performer. He gave only about 30 performances, many of which were private affairs. From 1838 to 1847 Chopin was romantically involved with novelist Georges Sand (Aurore Dudevant). The years of their stormy romance were his most productive as a composer. While Franz Lizst created works of grand proportions and brilliant virtuosity, Chopin remained a miniaturist, creating elegant, fluid melodies within the framework of small pieces. He was the only great composer who wrote almost exclusively for the piano. Chopin is set apart from other Romantic era composers by the fact that his works were not inspired by or based upon literature, works of art, or political ideals. Composition was difficult work for Chopin, who was a gifted improviser from his earliest days. He composed as he played, finding it painful to commit his work to paper. When Chopin and Georges Sand parted ways in 1847, the composer's frail health took a turn for the worse. He was further weakened by his 1848 concert tour of England. When he died in October of 1849, public fascination only increased, as evidenced by the nearly 3,000 mourners who attended his funeral.

FRANÇOIS COUPERIN (1668-1733)

Born into a musical family, it is probable that Couperin received his first music lessons from his father, who was an organist at St. Gervais in Paris. After his father's death, François was promised his post as organist which he attained upon reaching his eighteenth birthday. Couperin married into a well-connected family and both his music and career profited as a result. With a collection of organ pieces published and a new post as organist to Louis XIV in 1693, he began work on a set of sonatas inspired by the Italian Baroque master Corelli. At court, Couperin was a teacher of organ and harpsichord to the royal family. In 1717, he succeeded d'Anglebert to become the new harpsichordist to the king. During his time, Couperin was widely respected for his talents as teacher, performer and composer. In his music, he sought to marry the French and Italian styles, considered too difficult to achieve. His compositions include works for organ, harpsichord and chamber music, as well as both sacred and secular vocal music. In addition to having gained the respect and admiration of his contemporaries, Couperin was also revered by such great composers as Brahms, Richard Strauss, Debussy and Ravel.

CLAUDE DEBUSSY (1862-1918)

Claude Debussy saw rules as things to be tested. He repeatedly failed harmony exams during his student years, because of his refusal to accept that the rules were correct. Like many before him he took several tries to win the Priz de Rome. Debussy's musical language was affected by the music of Wagner (which he heard first-hand at the Bayreuth Festival) and Russian music. Another important event was exposure to the hazy harmonies of Javanese music. Yet the voice that he found was completely French. His music was as much a part of the Impressionist school of thought as the work of any painter. The composer also found his voice in periodic writings as a music critic. By breaking rules and composing in a style uniquely his own, Debussy led the way for a generation of French composers. His piano music was unlike anything the world had heard up until then, evoking a huge variety of sounds and harmonies from the keyboard. When Debussy died, after a long and painful battle with brain cancer, it seemed as though no one noticed. In fact, France was too consumed with war in 1918 to pause for the death of a composer, even the most important composer in the country.

6

GEORGE FRIDERIC HANDEL (1685-1759)

George Frideric Handel had the good sense to find a receptive audience for his music. Born Georg Händel, in Halle, Germany, the composer defied his father's wishes that he pursue law. He became known as a skilled keyboard player and respectable composer, and became a friend of the composer Georg Philipp Telemann. When his operas were not particularly well received in Hamburg, Händel moved on to Italy. In 1711 he moved on once again, this time to England. Two weeks after his arrival, the spectacle of his opera Rinaldo made him a famous man. The composer became a British citizen, changing the spelling of his name to suit his new nationality. The move to Britain proved fruitful, but life was not without its hardships. In 1715 he plunged from the height of success and popularity to absolute ruin. He not only survived, but rebuilt his reputation and once again achieved success. When it became apparent that he was played out as a composer of operas, he turned his attention to the oratorio, finding even greater success there than he had with his operas. He eventually lost his eyesight, which meant the end of his career as a composer. By then, his name firmly established, he turned his attention to conducting and performing as an organist. Messiah, certainly Handel's most famous work, was both the last piece of music he would conduct and the last he would hear. He collapsed shortly after conducting a Good Friday performance of the oratorio. He died the following morning. According to his wishes, he was buried in Westminster Abbey. A statue at his grave depicts him in front of his desk, with quill pen in front of him. Lying on the desk is a score of Messiah, open to the soprano aria, "I Know That My Redeemer Liveth."

JOHANN LUDWIG KREBS (1713-1780)

With a father as organist, Johann Ludwig Krebs received lessons at an early age. In the 1720s, he attended the Leipzig Thomasschule where he studied lute, keyboard and violin. Krebs had the good fortune of studying with J. S. Bach, who grew to hold the young Krebs in high esteem as both organist and composer. It was with Bach's recommendation that Krebs gained admission to the University of Leipzig in the 1730s. While attending the university, he balanced a demanding schedule and still found time to perform in Bach's collegium musicum as harpsichordist. Krebs worked as a copyist for Bach up until his mentor's death in 1750, at which time he applied for the vacant position at the Thomasschule, which he did not receive. It is clear by his focus on contrapuntal writing that Krebs was heavily influenced by the music of his teacher. The works of Johann Ludwig Krebs include pieces for keyboard, organ, voice and chamber ensemble.

FELIX MENDELSSOHN (1809-1847)

While most of Mendelssohn's colleagues could tell stories of their battles with family over choice of career and even more tales of their financial struggles as musicians, Felix Mendelssohn could only listen. He was born into a wealthy family that supported his goals in music from the very first. Even in their conversion from Judaism to Christianity, which the family had long considered, they were spurred to action by thoughts of their son's future. It was at the time of their conversion that they changed the family surname to Mendelssohn-Bartholdy. Mendelssohn set out on his musical career with two clear goals. He wanted to re-introduce the largely forgotten music of old masters such as Bach to the public, and he dreamed of opening a first-rate conservatory. At the age of twenty he conducted a pioneering performance of Bach's St. Matthew Passion, the first of many such concerts he would lead. A few years later he founded and directed the Leipzig Conservatory. As a composer, Mendelssohn combined the expressive ideals of the Romantics with the traditional forms of the Classical era. He is remembered both as one of the great Romantic composers and one of the last of classicists. In his career Mendelssohn found success at an early age, and remained highly successful until his death. His sister Fanny, to whom he was exceptionally close, died suddenly on May 14, 1847. Shortly after he got the news of his sister's death, Mendelssohn fell unconscious, having burst a blood vessel in his head. Although he recovered from this incident, he was terribly diminished by the illness. His health and mental state deteriorated until his death on November 4 that same year. Memorial services for the great conductor/composer were held in most German cities, as well as in various cities in Great Britain, where he had become quite a celebrity.

SERGEI PROKOFIEV (1891-1953)

As a boy, Sergei Prokofiev was arrogant and developed well beyond his years. This proved for a stormy childhood. Despite growing up in a remote part of the Ukraine, he was exposed to the latest developments in music through his teacher Glier, as well as his mother, a talented pianist. By the age of 12, Prokofiev had already composed a symphony and an opera, not to mention countless smaller works for piano. By the recommendation of Glazunov he applied and was accepted into the St. Petersburg Conservatory in 1904. There Prokofiev met his life-long friend Nicolay Myakovsky with whom he would attend the Evenings of Contemporary Music. It was at these concerts, which programmed works by Stravinsky, another Russian 'enfant terrible', that Prokofiev first came onto the scene as a composer-pianist. During the First World War, he composed his Classical Symphony, giving him an international reputation. Following a successful 10 year period of travel within the United States and Europe, Prokofiev returned to his native Russia, which by then had become the U. S. S. R. He was only occasionally allowed to tour outside the Soviet Union after that time. Prokofiev, among other composers, struggled against Soviet threats and censorship during the Stalin era. Prokofiev managed to hold onto his musical wit and energy despite unwelcoming times and all the changes in the world's musical fashions. Ironically enough, he passed away on the same day as Stalin, having suffered a brain hemorrhage.

HENRY PURCELL (1659-1695)

One of the greatest composers of the Baroque era and one of the greatest composers in English history, Henry Purcell found success in a wide range of musical formats. As the organist of Westminster Abbey and later the Chapel Royal, he composed and performed sacred music for services attended by British royalty as well as for public royal events. He turned his hand to theater music in about 1680. Since opera, as it was known in the rest of Europe, was not popular in England, he wrote incidental music for theatrical productions known as semi-operas. He wrote only one actual opera and one of the first written in the English language, *Dido and Aeneas*, for a girl's school in Chelsea. In addition to sacred music and music for royal events, Purcell wrote an enormous number of secular songs, many of which were published in songbooks during his lifetime. Although his works remained in publication and continued to be heard in performance (without the fall from public attention that the works of Bach and Vivaldi suffered), it was not until the 1878 formation of the Purcell Society that the composer's works were issued in a methodical, carefully catalogued fashion. Upon his death, Purcell was buried near the organ in Westminster Abbey, a clear indication of his position in British musical and religious circles. The last royal event for which Purcell composed music, was the funeral of Queen Mary in 1695. He died later that year.

SERGEI RACHMANINOFF (1873-1943)

Once described by composer Igor Stravinsky as "a six-and-a-half-foot-tall scowl," Sergei Rachmaninoff's stern visage was a trademark of sorts. Rachmaninoff first found fame as a pianist, touring throughout his native Russia to critical acclaim. His compositions won notice in those early years as well, including a Moscow Conservatory Gold Medal in composition. Yet the 1897 premiere of his Symphony No. 1 was a complete failure, due in large part to poor conducting by Alexander Glazunov. The dismal reception of the piece sent Rachmaninoff into a three-year creative slump that he overcame through hypnosis. During those three years he began conducting, earning international respect for his work on the podium. When his Symphony No. 1 received its London premiere in 1909, it was a huge success. Rachmaninoff made his first U.S. tour in 1909. On the tour he featured his Piano Concerto No. 3, which he had written expressly for his American audiences. Rachmaninoff fled Russia in the wake of the October Revolution of 1917. He brought his family to America where he continued to concertize, but did not compose for nearly a decade. After years of touring, Rachmaninoff decided that the 1942-43 concert season would have to be his last. In January of 1943 he began to suffer from an illness diagnosed as pleurisy. He gave what was to be his final performance on February 17. He then returned to his Beverly Hills home where he died of cancer on March 28.

CLARA SCHUMANN (1819-1896)

A pianist of technical mastery and a talented composer since childhood, Clara Wieck Schumann grew to become one of the most admired musical figures of her time. At the insistence of her father, Clara was given advanced musical education from an early age. Her virtuosity was noted by many great artists of the time including Goethe, Mendelssohn, Liszt and Pagannini. In 1828 Robert Schumann began piano studies with Friedrich Wieck, making the acquaintance of his nine-year-old daughter, Clara. As she matured, Schumann fell in love with her, despite the nine year age difference. Schumann and Clara eventually married, after a nasty legal battle against her father, who refused to give his consent for her to marry as a minor. Marriage brought joys and hardships for Clara. Despite raising children and attending to her husband's need for solace during composition, Clara found time to compose and to tour as a pianist. She was a strong advocate for new works of Brahms, Robert Schumann and Chopin; she premièred many herself. The young Johannes Brahms was taken in by the Schumanns in 1853. Robert's mental health declined, and he was institutionalized for two years until his death in 1856. Clara continued performing after his death, as well as holding positions on the faculties of the conservatories at Leipzig and Frankfurt. Always close, Clara and Brahms had developed a lifelong friendship, which many have speculated may have been romantic. Clara Schumann's compositions include works for piano, orchestra, and chamber ensembles, as well as many songs.

ALEXANDER SKRYABIN (1872-1915)

Pianist and composer Alexander Skryabin, a classmate of Rachmaninoff, is remembered for the unflinching modernism of his later works and for his mystical theories relating color to musical pitches. He was born into an aristocratic Russian family and was raised by an aunt, grandmother and great-aunt following the death of his mother. The women in Skryabin's life doted on him, catering to his every need and whim while fostering his egomaniacal, fastidious tendencies. In later years he depended on his managers for such catering. Skryabin was a short man, whose small hands were unable to reach more than an octave on the piano—a surprising fact, considering the reach required in some of his music. At the time of his death, which was caused by an infected boil on his lip, Skryabin had ambitious plans for a quasi-religious work entitled *Mysterium*. The work was intended to unite all of the various arts. Much of the music dating from the last four years of the composer's life was written in preparation for this piece, using floating dissonance of the "mystic" chord (C-F#-Bb-E-A-D). Much of Skryabin's earlier work was heavily influenced by the music of Chopin. As his own style developed he began to write more ornate and dissonant music, often making use of whole-tone passages and harmonies.

Preludio
from CANTOS DE ESPAÑA

Isaac Albéniz
1860–1909
Op. 232, No. 1

Allegro ma non troppo

marcato il canto

cresc.

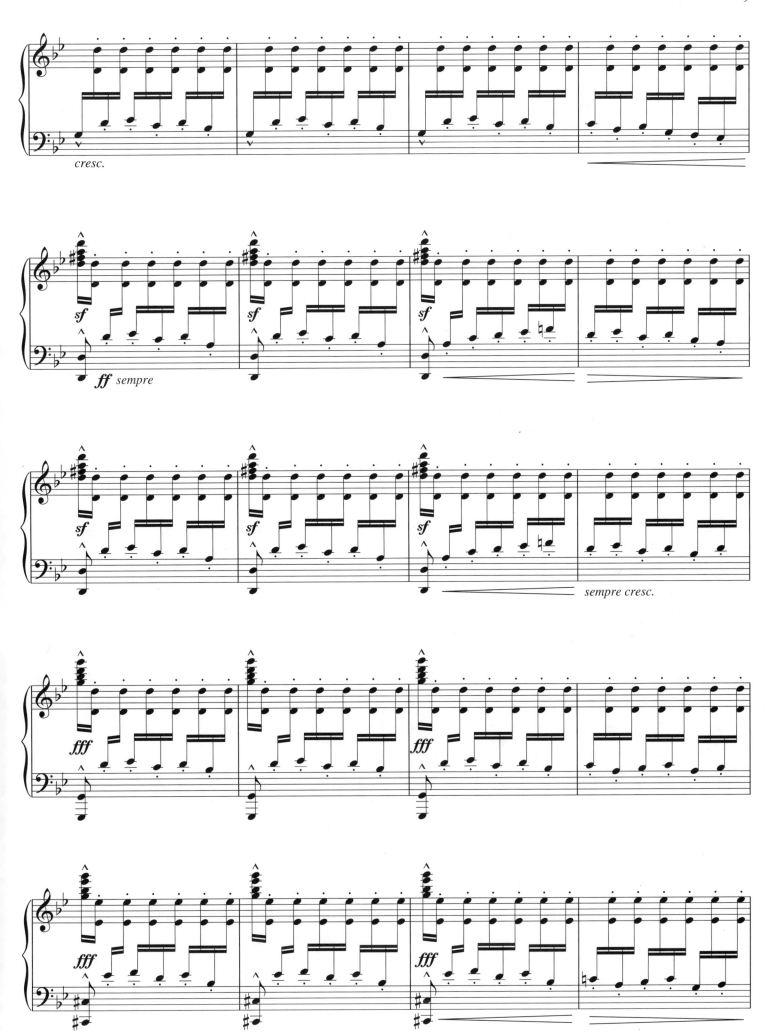

12

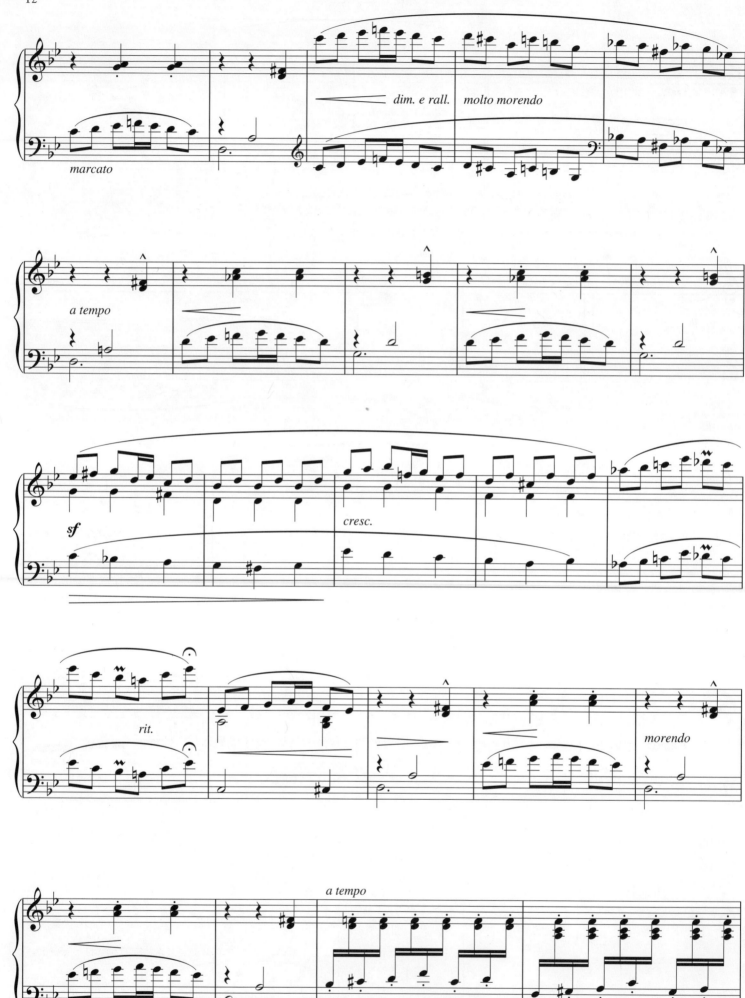

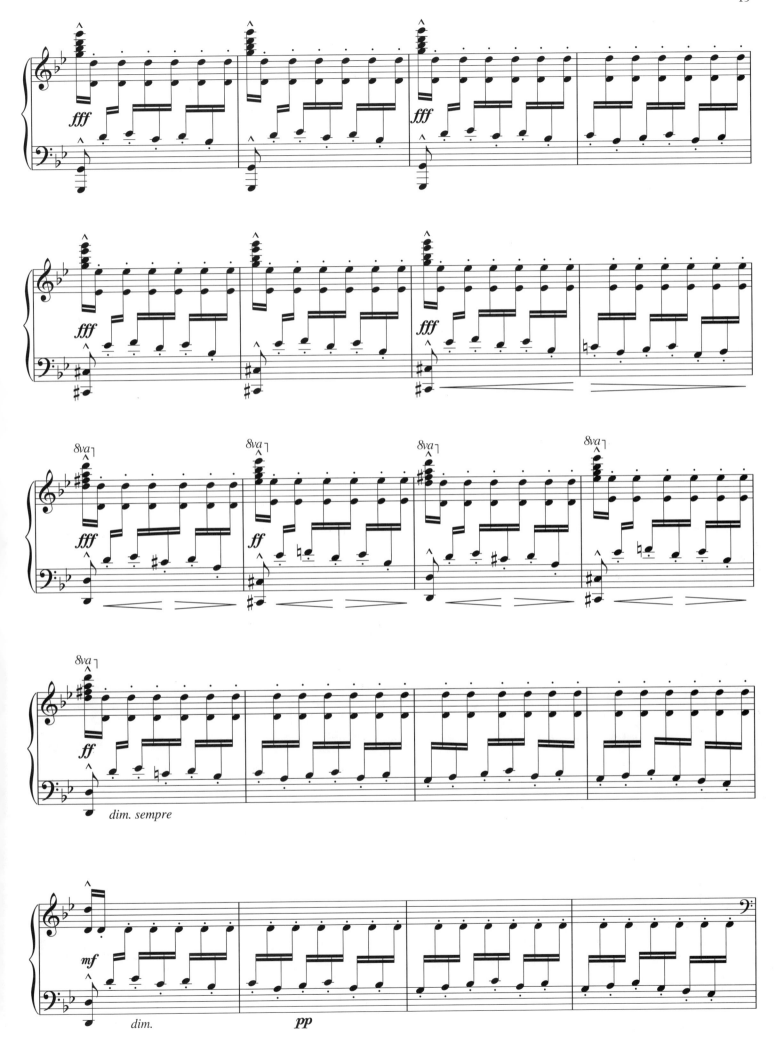

Preludio
from ESPAÑA

Isaac Albéniz
1860–1909
Op. 165, No. 1

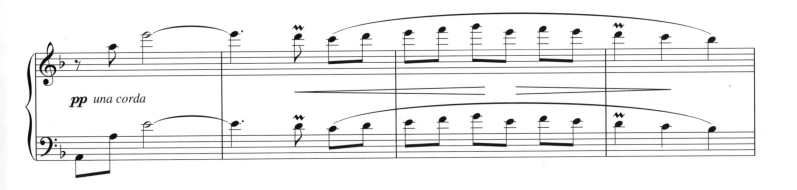

18

Prelude in B Major

Charles Valentin Alkan
1813–1888
Op. 31, No. 23

Quasi allegro ♩ = 120

Little Prelude No. 3 in C Minor
from 12 LITTLE PRELUDES

Johann Sebastian Bach
1685-1750

Little Prelude No. 4 in D Major

from 12 LITTLE PRELUDES

Johann Sebastian Bach
1685–1750

[Moderato]

Little Prelude No. 11 in G Minor

from *12 LITTLE PRELUDES*

Johann Sebastian Bach
1685–1750

Prelude in C Major
from THE WELL-TEMPERED CLAVIER, BOOK I

Johann Sebastian Bach
1685–1750
BWV 846

Prelude in D Minor
from THE WELL-TEMPERED CLAVIER, BOOK I

Johann Sebastian Bach
1685-1750
BWV 851

Prelude in C Minor
from THE WELL-TEMPERED CLAVIER, BOOK I

Johann Sebastian Bach
1685-1750
BWV 847

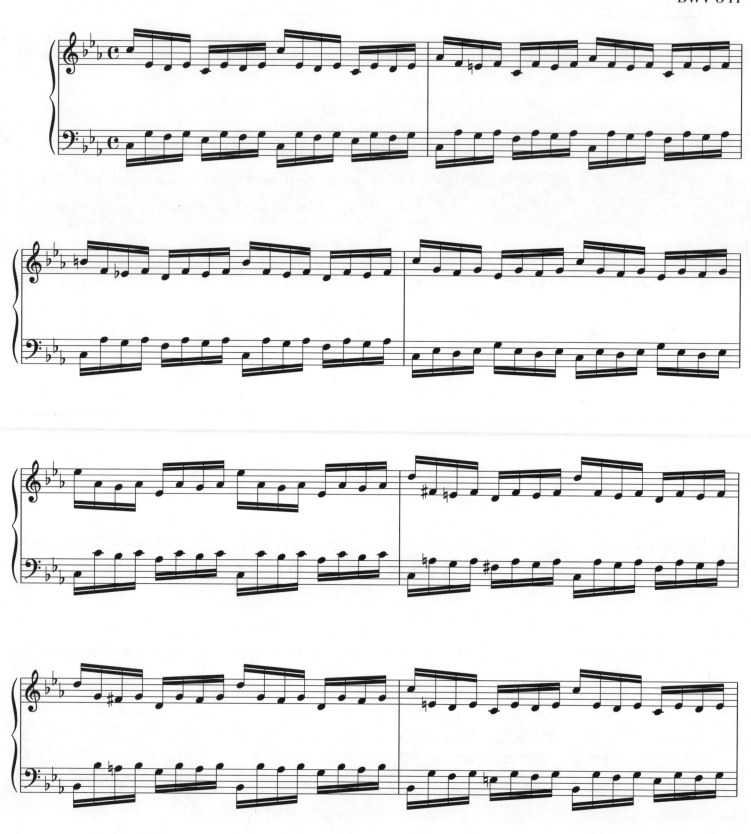

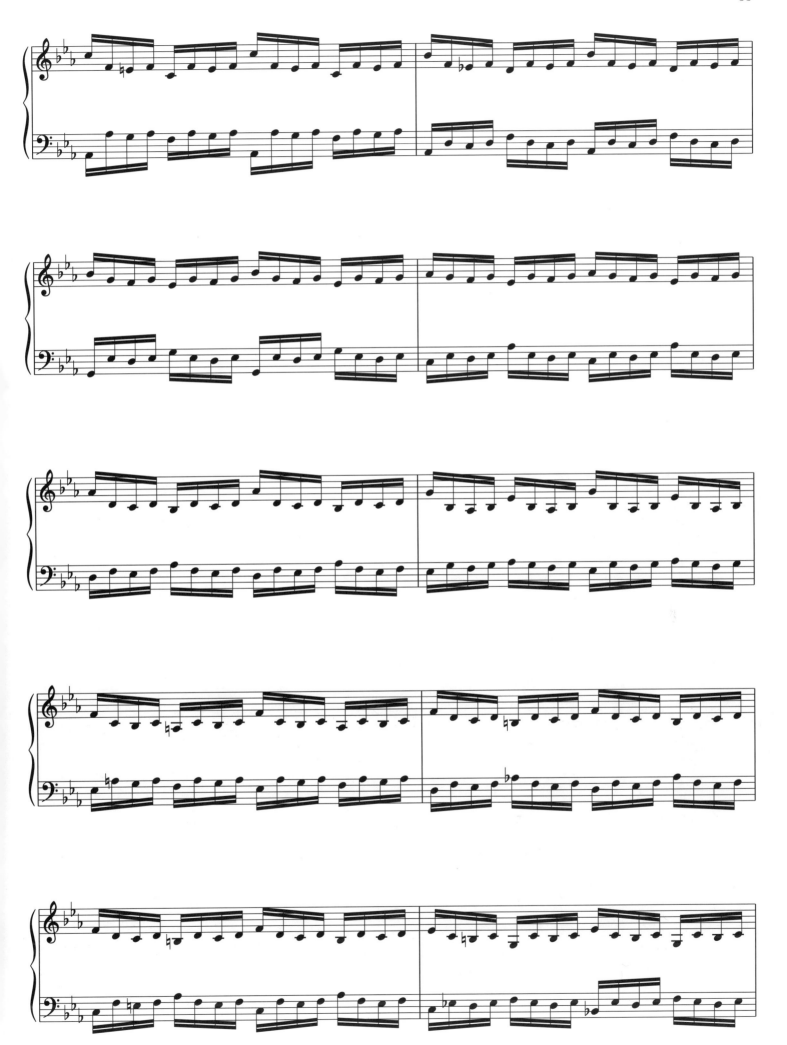

Presto

Prelude in D Major
from THE WELL-TEMPERED CLAVIER, BOOK I

Johann Sebastian Bach
1685-1750
BWV 850

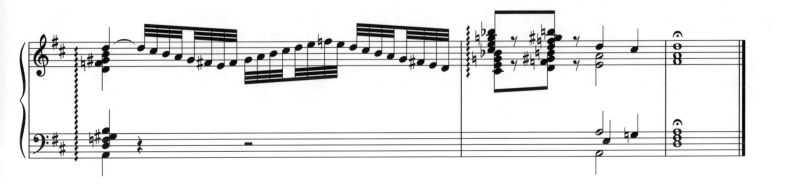

Prelude in G Major
from THE WELL-TEMPERED CLAVIER, BOOK I

Johann Sebastian Bach
1685–1750
BWV 860

Prelude in G Minor
from THE WELL-TEMPERED CLAVIER, BOOK I

Johann Sebastian Bach
1685-1750
BWV 861

Prelude in C Major
from THE WELL-TEMPERED CLAVIER, BOOK II

Johann Sebastian Bach
1685–1750
BWV 870

Prelude in D Major
from THE WELL-TEMPERED CLAVIER, BOOK II

Johann Sebastian Bach
1685–1750
BWV 874

Prelude in D Minor
from THE WELL-TEMPERED CLAVIER, BOOK II

Johann Sebastian Bach
1685–1750
BWV 875

Prelude in F Minor
from THE WELL-TEMPERED CLAVIER, BOOK II

Johann Sebastian Bach
1685–1750
BWV 881

Two Preludes through all Major Keys

1.

Ludwig van Beethoven
1770–1827
Op. 39

2.

Prelude in D-flat Major

Ferruccio Busoni
1866–1924
Op. 37, No. 15

Prelude in F-sharp Minor

Ferruccio Busoni
1866–1924
Op. 37, No. 8

Allegro moderato

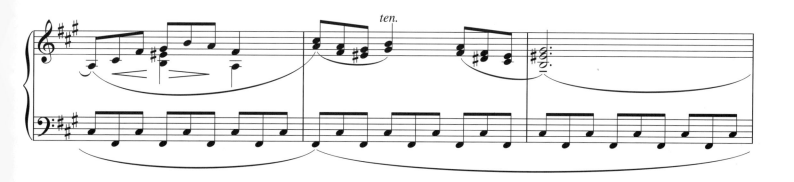

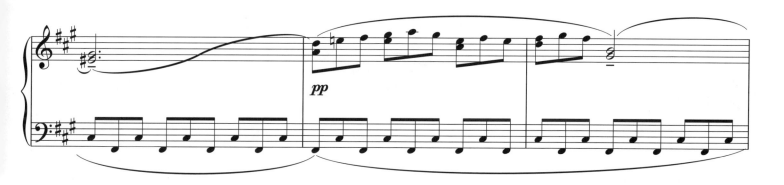

76

Prelude in A-flat Major

Fryderyk Chopin
1810–1849
Op. 28, No. 17

Prelude in A Major

Fryderyk Chopin
1810–1849
Op. 28, No. 7

Andantino

Prelude in B Minor

Fryderyk Chopin
1810-1849
Op. 28, No. 6

Lento assai

sotto voce

Prelude in C Minor

Fryderyk Chopin
1810–1849
Op. 28, No. 20

Largo

Prelude in C-sharp Minor

Fryderyk Chopin
1810–1849
Op. 45

Prelude in D-flat Major
("Raindrop")

Fryderyk Chopin
1810-1849
Op. 28, No. 15

Prelude in E Major

Fryderyk Chopin
1810–1849
Op. 28, No. 9

Prelude in F-sharp Major

Fryderyk Chopin
1810–1849
Op. 28, No. 13

Prelude in E Minor

Fryderyk Chopin
1810–1849
Op. 28, No. 4

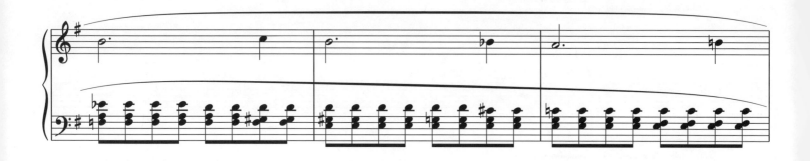

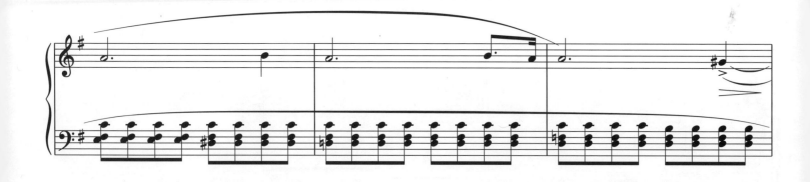

Prelude in G Minor

Fryderyk Chopin
1810–1849
Op. 28, No. 22

Molto agitato

Third Prelude
from L'ART DE TOUCHER LE CLAVECIN

François Couperin
1668−1733

Mesuré [Measured]

Eighth Prelude
from L'ART DE TOUCHER LE CLAVECIN

François Couperin
1668–1733

Mesuré - léger [Strict time - lightly]

La Cathédrale engloutie

(The Sunken Cathedral)

from PRÉLUDES, BOOK I

Claude Debussy
1862–1918

Peu à peu sortant de la brume

Un peu moins lent *(dans une expression allant grandissant)*

au Mouvement

pp *comme un écho de la phrase entendue précédemment*

Flottant et sourd.

8vb

(8vb)

(8vb)

più *p*

(8vb)

Dans la sonorité du début

8va

8va

8va

pp

(8vb)

Des pas sur la neige

from PRÉLUDES, BOOK I

Claude Debussy
1862-1918

La fille aux cheveux de lin
(The Girl with the Flaxen Hair)

Claude Debussy
1862-1918

Très calme et doucement expressif (♩ = 66)

Canope
from PRÉLUDES, BOOK II

Claude Debussy
1862–1918

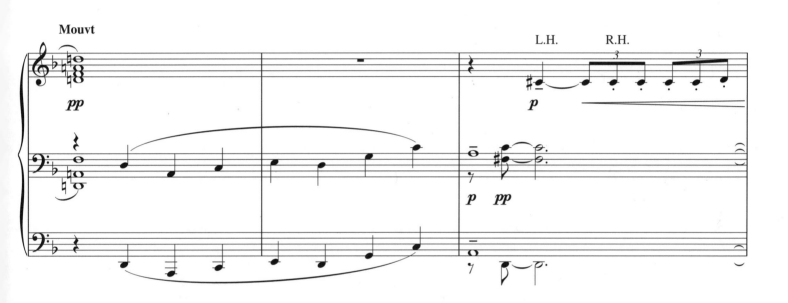

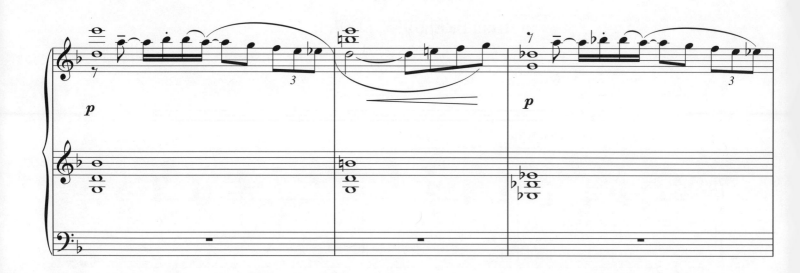

Animez un peu

Minstrels
from PRÉLUDES, BOOK I

Claude Debussy
1862–1918

au Mouvement

Bruyères
from PRÉLUDES, BOOK II

Claude Debussy
1862–1918

Calme – Doucement expressif

Prelude
from SUITE IN D MINOR

George Frideric Handel
1685–1759
HG II/i/3

Prelude
from SUITE IN E MAJOR

George Frideric Handel
1685–1759
HG II/i/5

Prelude
from SUITE IN F MINOR

George Frideric Handel
1685–1759
HG II/i/8

Prelude No. 3 in E Minor

Johann Ludwig Krebs
1713–1780

Prelude

Sergei Prokofiev
1891–1953
Op. 12, No. 7

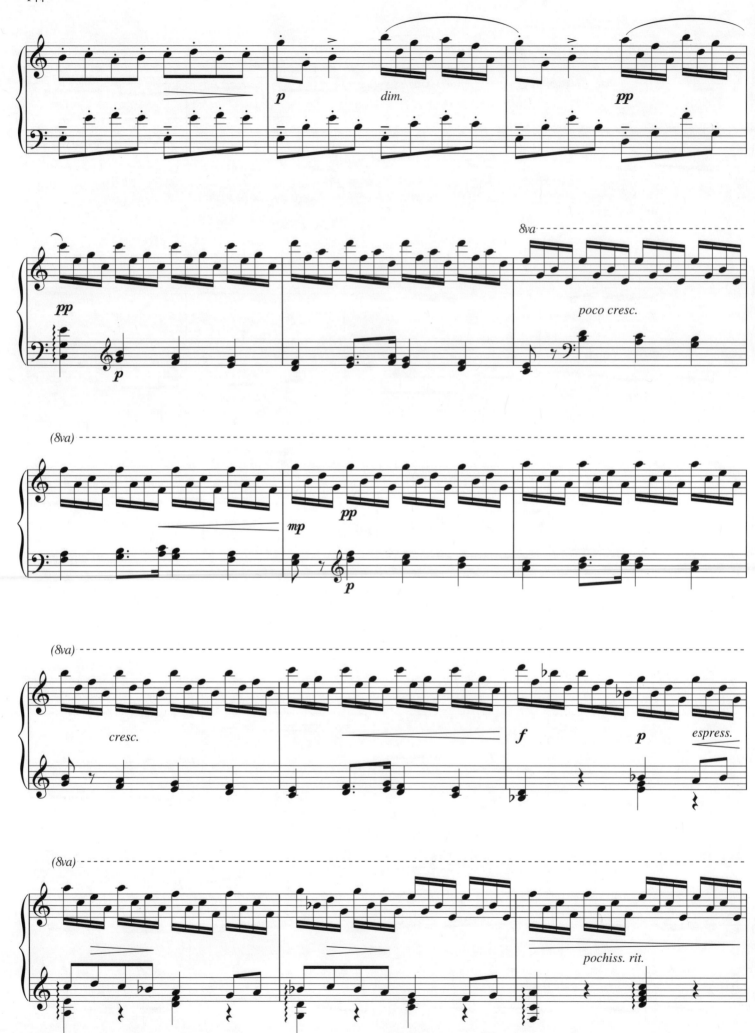

Prelude No. 5 in G Major

Johann Ludwig Krebs
1713–1780

Prelude No. 4 in A-flat Major

from SIX PRELUDES AND FUGUES

Felix Mendelssohn
1809–1847
Op. 35, No. 4

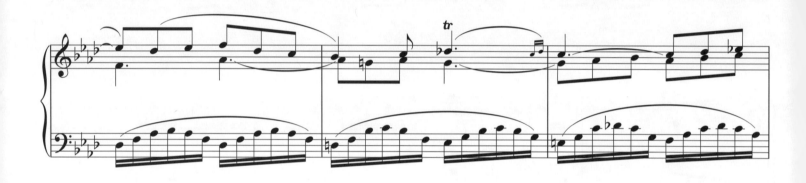

Prelude No. 5 in F Minor
from SIX PRELUDES AND FUGUES

Felix Mendelssohn
1809–1847
Op. 35, No. 5

Andante lento

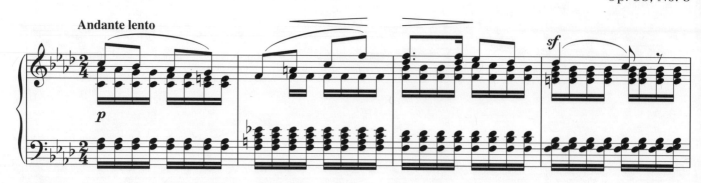

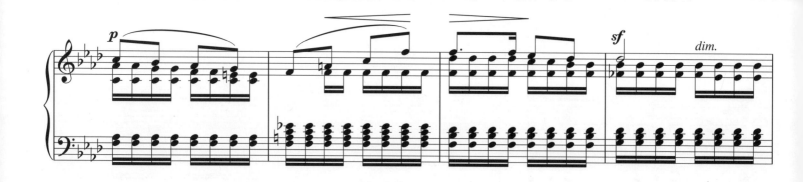

Prelude No. 6 in B-flat Major
from SIX PRELUDES AND FUGUES

Felix Mendelssohn
1809–1847
Op. 35, No. 6

Prelude
from SUITE IN C MAJOR

Henry Purcell
1659–1695
Z. 666

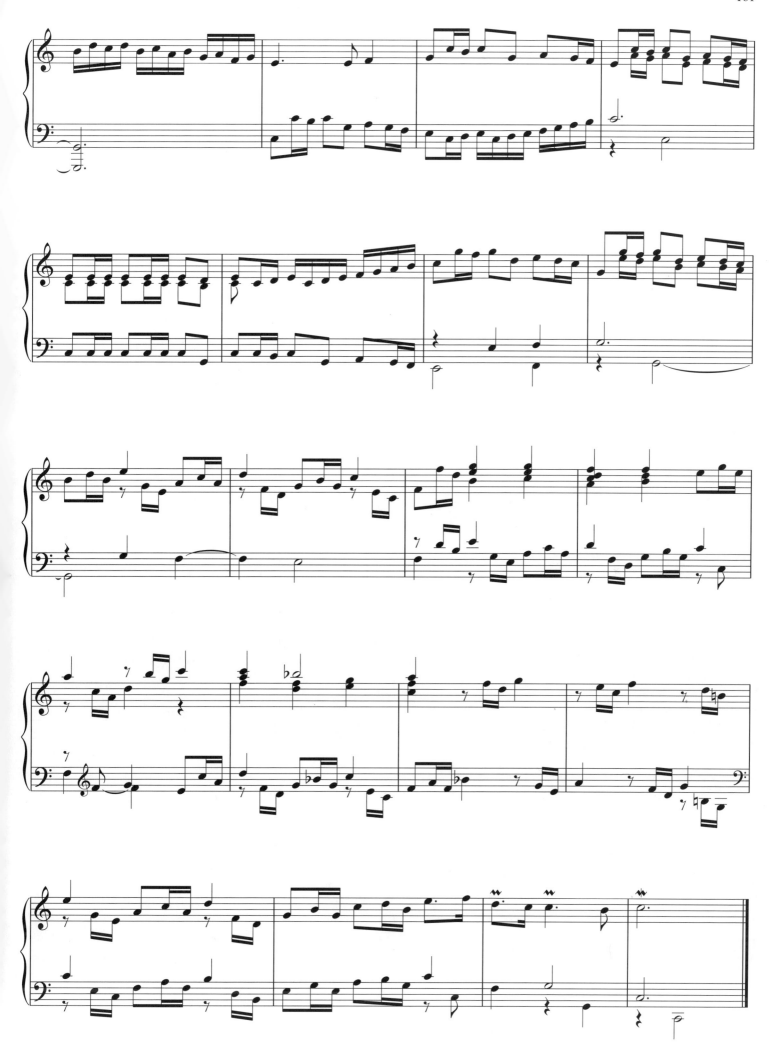

Prelude
from SUITE IN G MAJOR

Henry Purcell
1659–1695
Z. 662

Prelude
from SUITE IN G MINOR

Henry Purcell
1659–1695
Z. 661

Prelude in C-sharp Minor

Sergei Rachmaninoff
1873-1943
Op. 3, No. 2

Tempo I

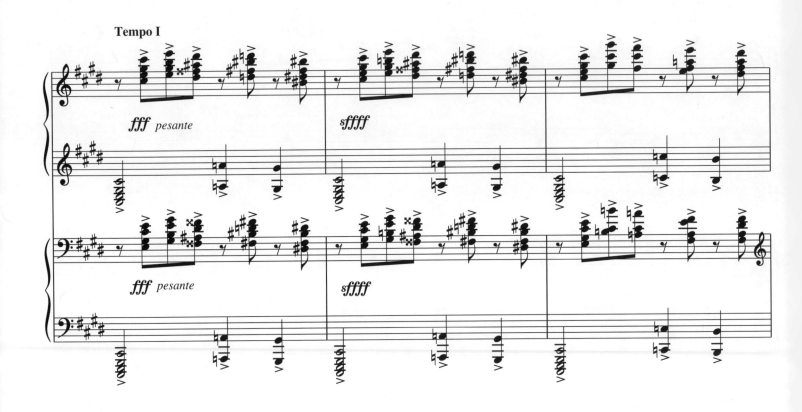

Prelude in D Major

Sergei Rachmaninoff
1873–1943
Op. 23, No. 4

174

Prelude in E-flat Major

Sergei Rachmaninoff
1873–1943
Op. 23, No. 6

Prelude in G Major

Sergei Rachmaninoff
1873-1943
Op. 32, No. 5

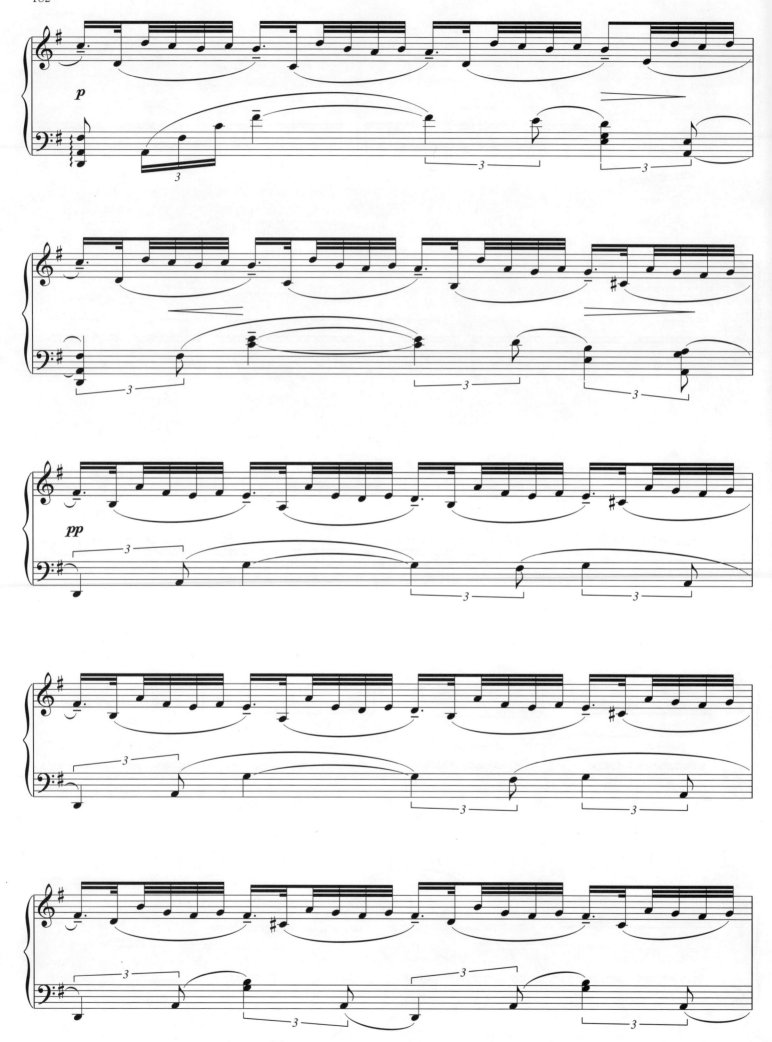

Prelude in G Minor

Sergei Rachmaninoff
1873–1943
Op. 23, No. 5

Prelude in G-sharp Minor

Sergei Rachmaninoff
1873–1943
Op. 32, No. 12

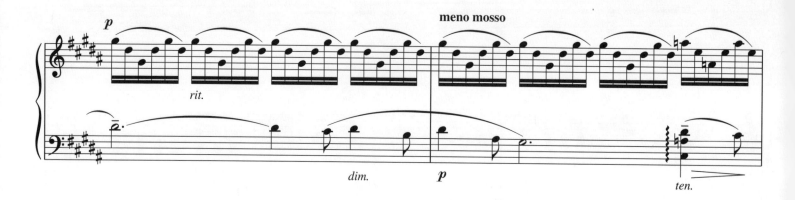

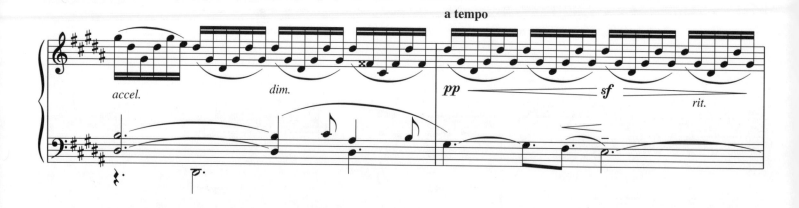

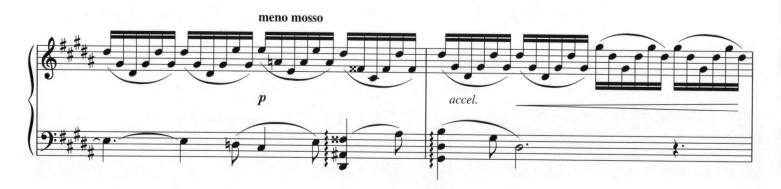

Prelude No. 2 in B-flat Major

from THREE PRELUDES AND FUGUES

Clara Schumann
1819-1896
Op. 16

Prelude for the Left Hand in C-sharp Minor

Alexander Skryabin
1872–1915
Op. 9, No. 1

Andante

Prelude in A Minor

Alexander Skryabin
1872–1915
Op. 11, No. 2

Prelude in C-sharp Minor

Alexander Skryabin
1872–1915
Op. 22, No. 2

Prelude in B-flat Major

Alexander Skryabin
1872–1915
Op. 35, No. 2

*Original edition reads B♮.

Prelude in E Major

Alexander Skryabin
1872–1915
Op. 11, No. 9

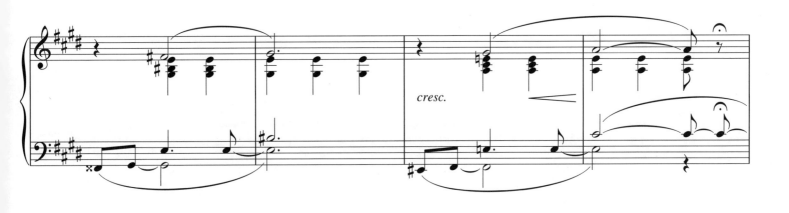

Prelude in G Major

Alexander Skryabin
1872–1915
Op. 11, No. 3

Prelude in G-sharp Minor

Alexander Skryabin
1872–1915
Op. 22, No. 1

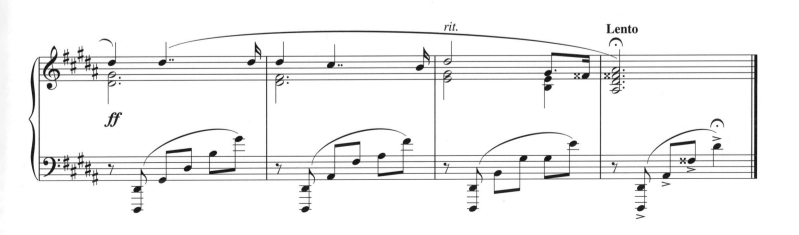